## Disclaimer

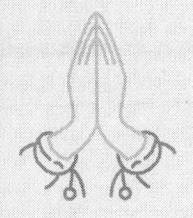

This fasting and prayer guide book incorporates biblical verses and references praise and worship songs with specific artists. Readers should be aware that personal interpretations of scripture and musical preferences are subjective. The inclusion of specific songs and artists does not imply endorsement or association. The author and publishers disclaim responsibility for individual interpretations and experiences related to the suggested songs. Users are encouraged to approach spiritual practices with discernment and consult spiritual leaders. The guide does not substitute professional advice. Readers with health concerns should seek professional guidance before engaging in fasting. Use of this guide indicates acknowledgment of individual responsibility for spiritual practices and experiences.

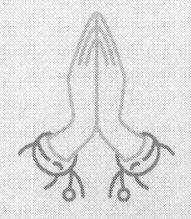

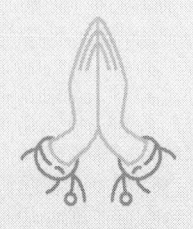

# Opening Heartfelt Prayer

Dear Heavenly Father,
In the quiet spaces of my heart, I humbly kneel before You as I embark on this sacred journey of fasting and prayer. In the simplicity of fasting, I seek the profound depth of Your presence. My heart is open, laid bare before You.
Lord, as I step into this season, I surrender not only my aspirations and hopes but also the vulnerabilities that lie within. In the simplicity of fasting, may my spirit be attuned to Your whisper, and may my humility be a fragrant offering in Your sight.
As I open this prayer and fasting guide, I invite Your Holy Spirit to be my intimate companion. Guide my reflections, illuminate the Scriptures, and shape my prayers into a melody that resonates with Your heart.
In the silent spaces between bites and in the surrender of sustenance, may I find sustenance in You. Strengthen me, not just physically but in the core of my being. May this journey be more than abstaining; may it be a deep communion with Your love.
Lord, in the echo of my heartbeat, hear the desires, fears, and dreams that I lay before You. In the simplicity of fasting, may I find the richness of Your grace. Your presence is my sustenance; Your love, my guiding light.
In the name of Jesus, whose humility inspires me, I embark on this fasting and prayer journey. May my heart be a vessel for Your transformative work.
Amen.

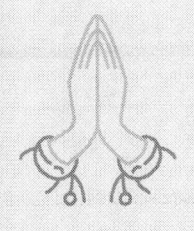

# Introduction to Fasting

Types of Fasts:
1. Complete Fast:
   - Definition: A complete fast involves abstaining from all forms of food and liquids for a specific period.
   - Biblical Reference: Esther 4:16 - Queen Esther called for a complete fast before approaching the king on behalf of her people.
2. Partial Fast:
   - Definition: In a partial fast, individuals limit their intake to specific types of food or exclude certain meals.
   - Biblical Reference: Daniel 1:12 - Daniel and his friends observed a partial fast by abstaining from the royal food and wine.
3. Daniel Fast:
   - Definition: The Daniel fast, inspired by Daniel's experiences in the Bible, typically involves abstaining from specific foods, like meat and sweets, and focusing on a plant-based diet.
   - Biblical Reference: Daniel 10:2-3 - Daniel's reference to abstaining from rich foods, meat, and wine during a time of mourning and seeking God's guidance.

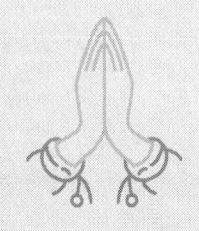

# Continuation

4. Intermittent Fast:
Alternating between periods of eating and fasting. Acts 13:2-3 - The early church practiced fasting while worshiping and seeking God's guidance.

5. Corporate Fast:
A group or community collectively engages in fasting. Joel 2:12 - The prophet Joel calls for a corporate fast, urging the people to return to God with fasting and mourning.

6. Liquid Fast:
Consuming only liquids while abstaining from solid food. Daniel 10:2-3 - Daniel abstained from rich foods, meat, and wine during a time of seeking God.

7. Sunrise to Sunset Fast:
Fasting from sunrise to sunset, commonly observed in some religious traditions. Matthew 4:2 - Jesus fasted for forty days and nights in the wilderness.

8. Religious Observance Fast:
Fasting as part of religious observances or rituals. Luke 18:12 - The Pharisee in Jesus' parable boasted about fasting twice a week as part of his religious practice.

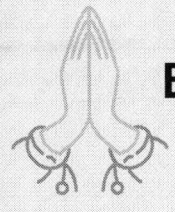

# Biblical References on Fasting

1. Matthew 6:16-18 (NIV):
   - "When you fast, do not look somber as the hypocrites do, for they disfigure their faces to show others they are fasting. Truly I tell you, they have their reward. But when you fast, put oil on your head and wash your face, so that it will not be obvious to others that you are fasting, but only to your Father, who is unseen; and your Father, who sees what is done in secret, will reward you."
2. Acts 13:2-3 (NIV):
   - "While they were worshiping the Lord and fasting, the Holy Spirit said, 'Set apart for me Barnabas and Saul for the work to which I have called them.' So after they had fasted and prayed, they placed their hands on them and sent them off."
3. Joel 2:12 (NIV):
   - "'Even now,' declares the Lord, 'return to me with all your heart, with fasting and weeping and mourning.'"
4. Luke 4:1-2 (NIV):
   - "Jesus, full of the Holy Spirit, left the Jordan and was led by the Spirit into the wilderness, where for forty days he was tempted by the devil. He ate nothing during those days, and at the end of them, he was hungry."
5. 2 Chronicles 7:14 (NIV):
   - "If my people, who are called by my name, will humble themselves and pray and seek my face and turn from their wicked ways, then I will hear from heaven, and I will forgive their sin and will heal their land."

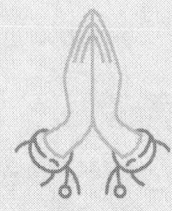

# Encouragement to Define Purpose for Fasting

Dear Reader,

As you embark on this sacred journey of fasting, take a moment to reflect on the purpose that fuels your commitment. Fasting is more than a physical act; it is a spiritual discipline that can deepen your connection with the divine.

Consider the following questions as you define your purpose:

1. What Spiritual Need Moves Your Heart? Identify the areas of your spiritual life that yearn for growth and transformation. Whether it's a desire for closer communion with God, seeking guidance, or experiencing breakthroughs, acknowledge these needs.
2. What Personal Challenges Are You Facing? Reflect on any personal challenges or obstacles that you wish to overcome. Fasting can serve as a powerful tool to confront and overcome struggles, fostering resilience and strength.
3. What Do You Hope to Learn About Yourself? Fasting provides a unique opportunity for self-discovery. Consider what aspects of your character, habits, or attitudes you want to explore during this time of intentional reflection.

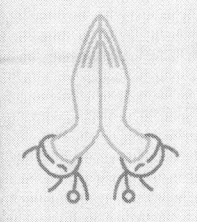

# Guidance on Setting Spiritual Goals

Once you've defined your purpose, translate it into tangible spiritual goals that will guide your journey:

1. Be Specific and Measurable: Clearly outline what you hope to achieve through fasting. Whether it's cultivating a habit of daily prayer, overcoming a particular temptation, or deepening your understanding of scripture, make your goals specific and measurable.
2. Align Goals with Your Purpose: Ensure that your spiritual goals directly align with the purpose you've defined for fasting. This alignment will give your journey a sense of cohesion and intentionality.
3. Prioritize Inner Transformation: While external outcomes are valuable, prioritize inner transformation. Consider goals related to cultivating virtues such as patience, gratitude, humility, or forgiveness.
4. Set Realistic Expectations: Be kind to yourself by setting realistic expectations. Fasting is a journey, and setting achievable goals ensures a sense of accomplishment and encouragement along the way.
5. Include Prayer and Reflection: Make prayer and reflection integral to your goals. Whether it's spending dedicated time in prayer, journaling, or engaging in spiritual reading, incorporate practices that nourish your soul.

Remember, your journey is unique, and your goals should reflect the personal nuances of your spiritual path. May this time of fasting be a profound and transformative experience, drawing you closer to the source of all grace and wisdom.

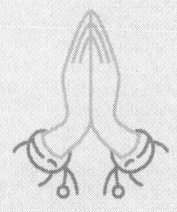

# Tips on Preparing Spiritually for a Fast

1. Set Clear Intentions: Before starting your fast, take time to set clear intentions and define your spiritual goals. Consider what you hope to achieve, whether it's seeking guidance, cultivating spiritual disciplines, or deepening your connection with God.
2. Pray for Guidance: Seek guidance through prayer before embarking on your fast. Ask for clarity, strength, and a receptive heart to fully engage in the spiritual journey ahead.
3. Reflect and Repent: Engage in self-reflection and repentance. Use this time to examine your heart, confess any shortcomings, and seek reconciliation with God. A repentant heart prepares the ground for spiritual transformation.
4. Plan Spiritual Practices: Integrate spiritual practices into your routine, such as reading scripture, meditating on verses, and incorporating prayer into your daily life. These practices will anchor your spirit during the fast.
5. Cultivate a Spirit of Gratitude: Approach your fast with a spirit of gratitude. Take time to acknowledge the blessings in your life, expressing thanks for God's goodness. Gratitude fosters a positive and receptive mindset.

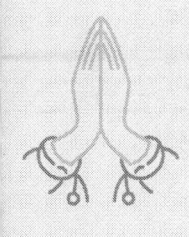

# Tips on Preparing Physically for a Fast

1. Gradual Transition: If you're new to fasting, consider a gradual transition. Start by reducing meal sizes or eliminating specific foods in the days leading up to the fast. This eases the body into the process.
2. Stay Hydrated: Hydration is crucial during a fast. Ensure you are well-hydrated in the days preceding the fast. Drink plenty of water to prepare your body for the temporary change in eating habits.
3. Balanced Nutrition: Consume a balanced and nutritious diet before the fast. Include a variety of fruits, vegetables, whole grains, and lean proteins. This provides essential nutrients that sustain your body during the fast.
4. Avoid Stimulants and Processed Foods: Minimize or eliminate the intake of stimulants like caffeine and processed foods. These can affect energy levels and may contribute to discomfort during the initial days of fasting.
5. Listen to Your Body: Pay attention to your body's signals. If you have any health concerns or conditions, consult with a healthcare professional before starting a fast. Listen to your body during the fast and adjust if needed.

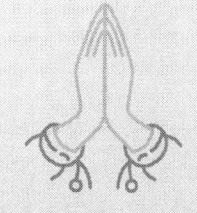

# Creating a Quiet Space for Prayer

1. Choose a Dedicated Space: Designate a specific area in your home as a sacred space for prayer. It could be a corner, a room, or even a comfortable chair where you feel a sense of tranquility.
2. Minimize Distractions: Create an environment free from distractions. Turn off electronic devices, choose a time when household activity is low, and let others know that you need some undisturbed time for prayer.
3. Include Meaningful Symbols: Enhance your quiet space with meaningful symbols such as candles, religious art, or items that hold spiritual significance. These can serve as visual reminders of your sacred time.
4. Use Soft Lighting: Opt for soft, calming lighting in your prayer space. This helps create a serene atmosphere conducive to reflection and prayer.
5. Incorporate Comfort: Make your prayer space comfortable. Use cushions, blankets, or a comfortable chair. Ensure that the temperature is conducive to a peaceful atmosphere.
6. Establish a Routine: Develop a routine for your prayer time. Consistency helps create a sense of ritual, signaling to your mind that it's time for sacred communion.

By preparing both spiritually and physically and creating a quiet space for prayer, you set the stage for a meaningful and transformative fasting experience. May this time be rich with spiritual insights and divine connection.

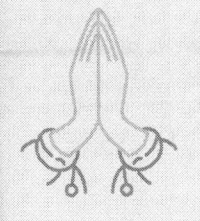

# Prayer Points

1. Commitment to the Journey:
   - Pray for unwavering commitment to the 40-day fast. Ask God for the strength to endure challenges and the discipline to stay focused on your spiritual goals.
2. Spiritual Hunger:
   - Seek a deeper hunger for God's presence and a thirst for His Word. Pray for a renewed passion for spiritual matters and a longing to draw nearer to Him.
3. Personal Transformation:
   - Pray for personal transformation during this extended period. Ask God to reveal areas in your life that need His healing touch and transformative power.
4. Guidance and Direction:
   - Seek God's guidance for decisions you may be facing during this season. Pray for clarity, wisdom, and discernment as you navigate life's challenges.
5. Intercession for Others:
   - Dedicate time to intercede for others. Lift up the needs of your family, friends, community, and the world. Pray for healing, reconciliation, and the spread of God's love.

Closing Prayer: Conclude your daily entry with a closing prayer. Express gratitude for the day, acknowledge God's presence in your journey, and surrender the upcoming days into His hands.

May your 40 days of prayer and fasting be a time of profound spiritual encounter, growth, and divine revelation. May you emerge from this journey strengthened in faith and closer to the heart of God.

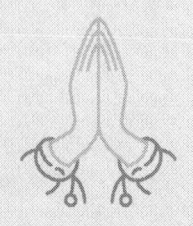

# Points of prayer

1. Adoration. Start by praising God for who He is.
2. Confession. Now, take some time to admit your wrongdoings. ...
3. Thanksgiving. Move into gratitude for every big and little thing you can think of. ...
4. Supplication. Finally, our spirits are prepared to ask God to meet our needs and desires.

Also.
   Pick a purpose: Matt 4:2, Mark 9:29.
   Stop eating : Matt 4:2-3, Daniel 10:2-3
   Keep it between you and God: Matt 6:18-18
      Pair Fasting with Prayers: Acts 14:23, Matt 17:21, Act 10:30 and 14:23, 1Corin 7:5.

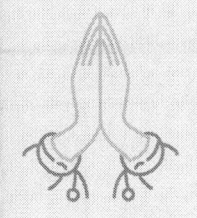

# Daily Reflections and Prayers

Reflection: Take a moment to reflect on the chosen verse and its relevance to your fasting journey. Consider the context, the message it conveys, and how it speaks to your current spiritual state. Allow the words to penetrate your heart and guide your thoughts throughout the day.

Prayer Points:
1. Personal Reflection: Pray for insight and revelation as you reflect on the verse in the context of your personal journey. Ask God to illuminate areas of your life that need His guidance and transformative touch.
2. Strength and Discipline: Seek God's strength to uphold you during the fast. Pray for discipline to remain committed to your spiritual goals, trusting that God's grace will sustain you.
3. Alignment with God's Will: Align your heart with God's will. Pray for the discernment to recognize His plans for you, and ask for the courage to surrender your desires and ambitions to His perfect purpose.
4. Spiritual Growth: Pray for spiritual growth during this fasting journey. Ask God to deepen your understanding of His Word, strengthen your faith, and mold you into the person He created you to be.
5. Gratitude and Praise: Express gratitude for the insights gained through the reflection on the verse. Praise God for His wisdom and the opportunity to draw nearer to Him through fasting.

Closing Prayer: Conclude your entry with a closing prayer. Thank God for the day, surrender your concerns and aspirations, and express your trust in His guidance throughout the remainder of the fasting journey.

# Warfare Prayer of Confession

Heavenly Father,
I humbly approach Your throne of grace, acknowledging the battles within and around me. I confess any sins, knowingly or unknowingly, that have given a foothold to the enemy in my life.
Scripture: Psalm 139:23-24 (NIV) "Search me, God, and know my heart; test me and know my anxious thoughts. See if there is any offensive way in me and lead me in the way everlasting."
I invite Your searching gaze into my heart, O God. Examine my thoughts and reveal any offensive ways within me. Lead me in the way everlasting.
Scripture: 1 John 1:9 (NIV) "If we confess our sins, he is faithful and just and will forgive us our sins and purify us from all unrighteousness."
I confess my sins before You, trusting in Your faithfulness and justice. Forgive me, Lord, and purify me from all unrighteousness.
Scripture: James 5:16 (NIV) "Therefore confess your sins to each other and pray for each other so that you may be healed. The prayer of a righteous person is powerful and effective."
I confess my sins not only before You but also to those around me. I seek healing through the power of Your forgiveness and the prayers of the righteous.
Now, as I lay bare my shortcomings before You, I ask for Your mercy and grace. Cleanse me, renew me, and fortify me for the spiritual battles ahead. In Jesus' name, I pray.
Amen.

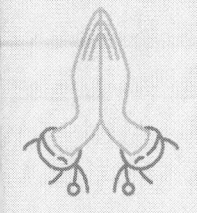

# Warfare Prayer of Salvation

Mighty God,
I come before Your throne with a heart that longs for salvation. I acknowledge my need for a Savior and declare my belief in Jesus Christ, Your Son, who died on the cross for my sins and rose again. I confess Him as my Lord and Savior.

Scripture: Romans 10:9-10 (NIV) "If you declare with your mouth, 'Jesus is Lord,' and believe in your heart that God raised him from the dead, you will be saved. For it is with your heart that you believe and are justified, and it is with your mouth that you profess your faith and are saved."
I declare with my mouth that Jesus is Lord, and I believe in my heart that You raised Him from the dead. I trust in His sacrifice for my justification and profess my faith in Him for salvation.

Scripture: John 3:16 (NIV) "For God so loved the world that he gave his one and only Son, that whoever believes in him shall not perish but have eternal life."
I receive the gift of eternal life offered through Your Son, Jesus Christ. I am grateful for Your boundless love and mercy.
Thank you, Father, for the salvation I find in Christ alone. Transform my heart, guide my steps, and fill me with Your Holy Spirit. In Jesus' name, I pray.
                Amen.

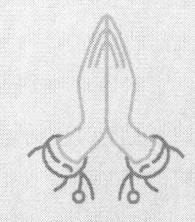

# Warfare Prayer of Pardon

Heavenly Father,
I approach Your throne with a contrite heart, recognizing my shortcomings and sins. I confess every transgression, both known and unknown, and seek Your forgiveness.

Scripture: 1 John 1:9 (NIV) "If we confess our sins, he is faithful and just and will forgive us our sins and purify us from all unrighteousness."
Father, I acknowledge my need for Your mercy and pardon. Wash me clean, purify my heart, and grant me the assurance of Your forgiveness through the precious blood of Jesus Christ.

Scripture: Psalm 51:10 (NIV) "Create in me a pure heart, O God, and renew a steadfast spirit within me."
Create within me a new heart, O God, and renew a steadfast spirit within me. Let Your mercy triumph over judgment, and may Your grace abound in my life.

Scripture: Psalm 103:12 (NIV) "As far as the east is from the west, so far has he removed our transgressions from us."
Thank You for removing my sins as far as the east is from the west. I receive Your pardon, and I choose to walk in the freedom You provide.
Father, I commit to turning away from sin and following Your ways. Fill me with Your Spirit, that I may live a life pleasing to You.
In the mighty name of Jesus, I pray.
    Amen.

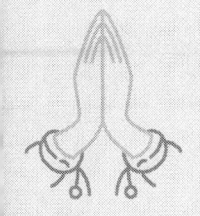

# Warfare Prayer of Promise

Heavenly Father,
As I stand in the midst of spiritual warfare, I find refuge and strength in the promises of Your Word. Your divine power has equipped me with everything I need for a godly life. Through the knowledge of You who called me by Your glory and goodness, I partake in Your precious promises, escaping the corruption of worldly desires.

I declare Isaiah 41:10 over my life: "Do not fear, for I am with you; do not be dismayed, for I am your God. I will strengthen you and help you; I will uphold you with my righteous right hand." In the face of spiritual battles, I reject fear, knowing that Your presence strengthens and upholds me.
Philippians 4:13 becomes my anthem: "I can do all this through him who gives me strength." In the arena of spiritual warfare, I affirm that my strength comes from Christ, enabling me to face challenges victoriously.

Romans 8:37 resonates within me: "No, in all these things we are more than conquerors through him who loved us." I embrace the truth that through Your love, I am not just a conqueror but more than a conqueror. Your love empowers me to triumph over every tactic of the enemy.
Lord, I hold fast to Your promises as a shield against the assaults of darkness. Your Word illuminates my path and guides me through the complexities of spiritual warfare. As I engage in this battle, I trust in the authority of Your promises to lead me to victory.
In the mighty name of Jesus, I pray.
            Amen.

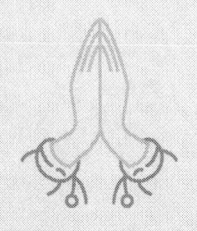

# Warfare Prayer of Submission

Heavenly Father,
In the battlefield of spiritual warfare, I come before Your throne with humility and surrender. I acknowledge Your sovereignty over all realms, seen and unseen. I submit every area of my life to Your divine authority.
Scripture assures me in James 4:7, "Submit yourselves therefore to God. Resist the devil, and he will flee from you." Father, I willingly submit my thoughts, emotions, and actions to Your guidance. I resist the schemes of the enemy, knowing that Your power within me is greater.
As Ephesians 6:13 encourages, I put on the full armor of God to stand firm against the strategies of the devil. Clothed in Your truth, righteousness, peace, faith, salvation, and the Word, I am equipped to withstand any spiritual assault.
I declare Romans 12:1-2 over my life: "I appeal to you therefore, brothers, by the mercies of God, to present your bodies as a living sacrifice, holy and acceptable to God, which is your spiritual worship. Do not be conformed to this world, but be transformed by the renewal of your mind."
I surrender my entire being as a living sacrifice, seeking transformation through the renewing of my mind by Your Word and Spirit. I renounce any alignment with the patterns of this world and choose to be conformed to Your will.
Lord, I yield my plans, desires, and ambitions to Your perfect purpose. Grant me discernment to recognize the subtle workings of the enemy and the strength to resist. May my submission to Your authority become a shield that deflects every attack of the adversary.
In the name of Jesus, I submit myself completely.
Amen.

# Warfare Prayer of Praise

Almighty God,
In the midst of spiritual battles, I lift my voice in praise to You. You are the Alpha and Omega, the Creator of all things, and the Sovereign Lord of the universe. I declare Your majesty and proclaim Your victory over every principality and power.

As the Psalmist exclaims in Psalm 47:1, "Clap your hands, all peoples! Shout to God with loud songs of joy!" Today, I choose to celebrate Your greatness, acknowledging that the enemy trembles at the sound of praises.

Your Word assures me in Psalm 22:3 that You inhabit the praises of Your people. In this moment, I invite Your divine presence to fill my surroundings as I offer heartfelt worship. I declare the truth of Psalm 149:6-7, "Let the high praises of God be in their throats and two-edged swords in their hands, to execute vengeance on the nations and punishments on the peoples."

Lord, I wield the weapon of praise as a two-edged sword against the forces of darkness. In the name of Jesus, I praise You for Your faithfulness, goodness, and unfailing love. I magnify Your name, knowing that Your glory dispels the schemes of the enemy.

As I praise You, Lord, let the atmosphere shift, and let Your angels encamp around me for protection. I trust that my praise is a powerful weapon, demolishing strongholds and ushering in Your triumphant presence.

May my praises echo in the heavens and resonate in the spiritual realm. I surrender every battle to You, O God, confident that in the midst of praise, Your victory is proclaimed. In Jesus' mighty name, I praise and worship.
Amen.

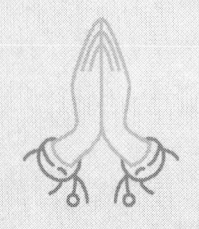

# Warfare Prayer for Blessing

Heavenly Father,
I come before Your throne in the authority of Jesus' name, acknowledging Your sovereignty over all things. As Your child, I declare my allegiance to You, my King and Provider. I stand on the promises of Your Word, believing that You desire to bless and prosper Your children.
Your Word in Numbers 6:24-26 declares, "The Lord bless you and keep you; the Lord make his face to shine upon you and be gracious to you; the Lord lift up his countenance upon you and give you peace." Today, I claim this divine blessing over my life, family, and endeavors.
In Deuteronomy 28:2, You promised, "All these blessings shall come upon you and overtake you if you obey the voice of the Lord your God." I commit to obeying Your voice, seeking Your will, and aligning my life with Your purposes.
I rebuke any hindrance or opposition that may stand against the blessings You have ordained for me. In the name of Jesus, I break the power of any curse, negativity, or spiritual opposition that seeks to block Your favor in my life.
Lord, as I meditate on Your Word day and night (Psalm 1:2-3), I trust that I will be like a tree planted by streams of water, yielding fruit in its season. Your promise in Psalm 23:6 reassures me: "Surely goodness and mercy shall follow me all the days of my life, and I shall dwell in the house of the Lord forever." I pray for a supernatural outpouring of Your blessings—financial, spiritual, emotional, and physical—upon my life. May Your favor be a shield around me (Psalm 5:12), and let the favor of the Lord my God be upon me; establish the work of my hands (Psalm 90:17).
Thank You, Lord, for Your abundance, and I receive these blessings with gratitude and humility. In Jesus' name, I pray.
Amen.

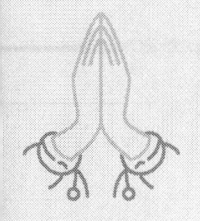

# Warfare Prayer!!!

Heavenly Father,

As I enter this battlefield of spiritual warfare, I stand clothed in the armor of Your Word (Ephesians 6:10-18). In the name of Jesus, I declare war against the forces of darkness that seek to hinder Your purpose in my life.

With the authority bestowed upon me by Christ (Luke 10:19), I rebuke every plan of the enemy to steal, kill, or destroy (John 10:10). Let the power of the blood of Jesus dismantle and render ineffective every demonic scheme devised against me (Revelation 12:11).

I raise a standard against the principalities and powers opposing me (Isaiah 59:19). By faith, I deploy the sword of the Spirit, which is Your Word, to cut through every stronghold (Hebrews 4:12). I release the fire of the Holy Spirit to consume and purify my environment (Matthew 3:11).

Lord, as I engage in this warfare, fill me with discernment and wisdom (1 Corinthians 2:14). Let the light of Your truth expose every hidden agenda of the enemy (Ephesians 5:11). I affirm that no weapon formed against me shall prosper (Isaiah 54:17).

In the shelter of Your presence, I find refuge and strength (Psalm 91:1-2). May the angelic hosts surround and protect me as I advance in this spiritual battle (Psalm 34:7).

In the matchless name of Jesus, I declare victory over every adversary.

    Amen.

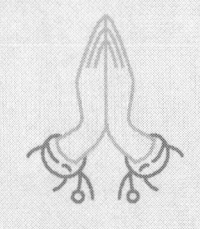

# Day 1: PRAYING EFFECTIVELY

Adoration.
Start by praising God for who He is.
Songs: " All To Jesus I Surrender" - Hillsong

Heavenly Father,
As we embark on this sacred journey of fasting and prayer, we come before You, inspired by the wisdom and promises found in Your Word. In Jeremiah 29:11-13, we cling to the assurance that Your plans for us are filled with hope and a future. We seek You earnestly, knowing that when we seek with all our hearts, we will find You.

Drawing strength from Ezra 8:21, we set our faces to seek You for guidance and protection throughout this fasting period. As we humble ourselves before You, we declare that our trust is in You alone, recognizing that Revelation 1:4-6 establishes You as the faithful witness and ruler of all.

Mark 11:22-26 teaches us the power of faith. Strengthen our faith, Lord, so that we may move mountains and experience breakthroughs during this time of fasting and prayer. Like the birds of the air, may we trust in Your provision, as stated in Matthew 6:31-34, for our daily needs.

## Day 1: continuation

In Isaiah 55:6-9, we are reminded of Your thoughts being higher than ours. Grant us the humility to surrender our understanding to Your divine wisdom. We embrace the challenge presented in Isaiah 58:3-8, seeking a genuine fast that leads to justice, mercy, and a closer walk with You.

Lord, as we meditate on these scriptures, may Your Word dwell richly in our hearts. We surrender every aspect of our lives to You, knowing that Your plans are perfect and Your mercy is abundant. Transform us into vessels of Your grace as we devote ourselves to fasting and prayer. In Jesus' name, we pray. Amen.

SPACE FOR PERSONAL REFLECTIONS, THOUGHTS, AND PRAYERS.

NOTES

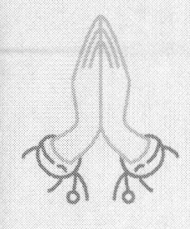

# Day 2: Prayer of Repentance and Forgiveness

Adoration.
Start by praising God for who He is.
Songs: "Mercy Seat" - Vicki Yohe

As I embark on this journey of fasting and prayer, I recognize the depth of my need for Your mercy and forgiveness. Your promise in 1 John 1:9 encourages me that if I confess my sins during this season of fasting, You are faithful and just to forgive and cleanse me.

Scripture: Psalm 51:10-11 (NIV)"Create in me a pure heart, O God, and renew a steadfast spirit within me. Do not cast me from your presence or take your Holy Spirit from me."
In the midst of my fasting, I humbly echo the words of David in Psalm 51, asking You to create in me a clean heart. As I abstain from physical nourishment, I seek a spiritual renewal—a steadfast spirit that remains focused on Your presence.

Scripture: Isaiah 58:6-7 (NIV)"Is not this the kind of fasting I have chosen: to loose the chains of injustice and untie the cords of the yoke, to set the oppressed free and break every yoke? Is it not to share your food with the hungry and to provide the poor wanderer with shelter—when you see the naked, to clothe them, and not to turn away from your own flesh and blood?"
Lord, as I fast, may my actions align with the type of fasting You desire—loosing the chains of injustice, setting the oppressed free, and extending compassion to those in need. May this fasting season be marked not only by personal repentance but by acts of justice and mercy.

## Day 2: continuation

Scripture: Daniel 9:3 (NIV) "So I turned to the Lord God and pleaded with him in prayer and petition, in fasting, and in sackcloth and ashes."

Following the example of Daniel, I turn to You, O Lord, in prayer and fasting. I come with a contrite heart, acknowledging my sins and seeking Your forgiveness. In this time of fasting, may my petitions be heard, and may Your mercy prevail.

Scripture: Matthew 6:16-18 (NIV) "When you fast, do not look somber as the hypocrites do, for they disfigure their faces to show others they are fasting. Truly I tell you, they have received their reward. But when you fast, put oil on your head and wash your face, so that it will not be obvious to others that you are fasting, but only to your Father, who is unseen; and your Father, who sees what is done in secret, will reward you."

As I engage in this fasting journey, I seek to do so with sincerity and a heart focused on You. May my fasting be a private expression of repentance and seeking Your face, and may You reward it with Your presence.

In the name of Your Son, Jesus Christ, who makes all things new, I pray.

Amen.

SPACE FOR PERSONAL REFLECTIONS, THOUGHTS, AND PRAYERS.

NOTES

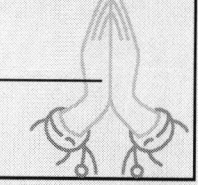

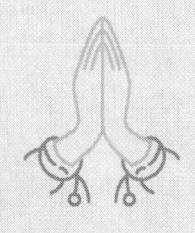

# Day 3: Prayer of Humility and Reconciliation

Adoration.
Start by praising God for who He is.
Songs: "Reckless Love" - Cory Asbury

Heavenly Father,
As I embark on this season of fasting, I recognize the importance of humility and reconciliation in the light of Your Word. During this time of denying myself physical comforts, I seek to embrace the virtues of humility and reconciliation.

Scripture: Philippians 2:3-4 (NIV)"Do nothing out of selfish ambition or vain conceit. Rather, in humility, value others above yourselves, not looking to your own interests but each of you to the interests of the others."
In the spirit of selflessness, Lord, I pray for humility. May this season of fasting be marked by valuing others above myself, considering their needs, and aligning my heart with the interests of those around me.

Scripture: Matthew 5:23-24 (NIV)"Therefore, if you are offering your gift at the altar and there remember that your brother or sister has something against you, leave your gift there in front of the altar. First, go and be reconciled to them; then come and offer your gift."
In the process of fasting, may my heart be prompted to seek reconciliation where needed. If there are broken relationships, grant me the humility to initiate reconciliation before offering my sacrifices to You.

# Day 3: continuation

Scripture: Colossians 3:12 (NIV)"Therefore, as God's chosen people, holy and dearly loved, clothe yourselves with compassion, kindness, humility, gentleness, and patience."
As I fast, clothe me, Lord, with virtues that reflect Your character—compassion, kindness, gentleness, and patience. May humility be the garment I wear during this fasting season.

Scripture: Ephesians 4:2-3 (NIV)"Be completely humble and gentle; be patient, bearing with one another in love. Make every effort to keep the unity of the Spirit through the bond of peace."
Lord, in this time of fasting, make me completely humble and gentle. Grant me patience to bear with others in love. May my efforts be directed towards maintaining unity and fostering peace in the Spirit.
In the name of Jesus, the Prince of Peace, I pray.
                    Amen.

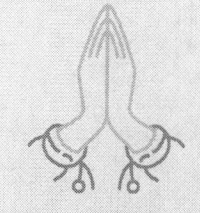

SPACE FOR PERSONAL REFLECTIONS,
THOUGHTS, AND PRAYERS.

NOTES

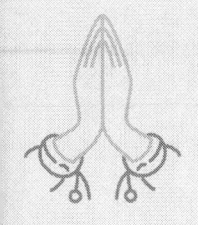

# Day 4 : Prayer of Honoring & Fearing God

Adoration.
Start by praising God for who He is.
Songs: "10,000 Reasons (Bless the Lord)" - Matt Redman
"You Are Alpha & Omega" - Israel & The New Breed

Heavenly Father,
As I bow before Your majestic presence, I am reminded of the profound significance of honoring and fearing You. Your Word declares in Proverbs 9:10, "The fear of the Lord is the beginning of wisdom, and knowledge of the Holy One is understanding." I acknowledge Your sovereignty, recognizing that true wisdom begins with a reverential awe of You.

Scripture: Psalm 111:10 (NIV) "The fear of the Lord is the beginning of wisdom; all who follow his precepts have good understanding. To him belongs eternal praise."
Lord, I embark on this journey of honoring and fearing You, understanding that it is the foundation of true wisdom. I seek wisdom that aligns with Your precepts, knowing that it leads to understanding and eternal praise.

Scripture: Ecclesiastes 12:13 (NIV) "Now all has been heard; here is the conclusion of the matter: Fear God and keep his commandments, for this is the duty of all mankind."
Father, I recognize that fearing You and keeping Your commandments are the essence of human existence. As I navigate this fasting and prayer season, instill in me a deep sense of duty to fear You and align with Your divine commands.

# Day 4: continuation

Scripture: Proverbs 3:7 (NIV) "Do not be wise in your own eyes; fear the Lord and shun evil."
God, help me to abandon my own wisdom and lean on Yours. Grant me the grace to fear You and turn away from all that is evil. May my actions and thoughts reflect a heart that truly honors You.
Scripture: Psalm 34:9 (NIV) "Fear the Lord, you his holy people, for those who fear him lack nothing."
Lord, I join the assembly of Your holy people, acknowledging that those who fear You lack nothing. May my fear of You open the floodgates of Your abundant blessings in every area of my life.
Scripture: Proverbs 22:4 (NIV) "Humility is the fear of the Lord; its wages are riches and honor and life."
Father, I embrace humility as an expression of my fear of You. I trust that humility will lead to riches, honor, and a life that glorifies Your name. In this journey, let humility be my constant companion.

Scripture: Malachi 3:16 (NIV) "Then those who feared the Lord talked with each other, and the Lord listened and heard. A scroll of remembrance was written in his presence concerning those who feared the Lord and honored his name."
God, create a fellowship among those who fear You during this season. May our conversations be pleasing to You, and let our names be written in Your scroll of remembrance. Grant us the grace to honor Your name in all we do.
In Jesus' precious name, I pray.
.                              Amen.

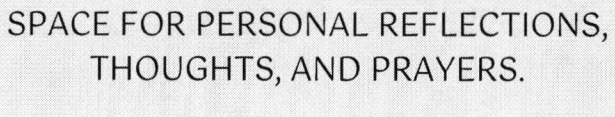

SPACE FOR PERSONAL REFLECTIONS, THOUGHTS, AND PRAYERS.

NOTES

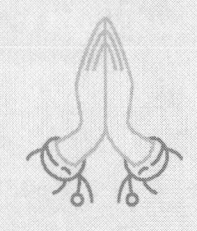

# Day 5 : Prayer for Building Your Faith

Adoration.
Start by praising God for who He is.
Songs: "Great Are You Lord" - All Sons & Daughters

Heavenly Father,
As I stand before You, I recognize the paramount importance of building and fortifying my faith. Your Word in Romans 10:17 declares, "So faith comes from hearing, and hearing through the word of Christ." I embark on this sacred journey of fasting and prayer with a fervent desire to strengthen my faith through the profound revelation of Your Word.
Scripture: Hebrews 11:1 (NIV) "Now faith is confidence in what we hope for and assurance about what we do not see."
Lord, I long to possess a faith that stands as a firm foundation, confident in the hope I have in You and assured of the unseen realities of Your promises. Strengthen my faith, I pray.
Scripture: Romans 10:17 (NIV) "Consequently, faith comes from hearing the message, and the message is heard through the word about Christ."
Father, as I immerse myself in the Word about Christ during this fasting and prayer season, let faith spring forth within me. May the revelation of Your truth ignite a profound faith that transforms every aspect of my life.
Scripture: James 1:6 (NIV) "But when you ask, you must believe and not doubt, because the one who doubts is like a wave of the sea, blown and tossed by the wind."
God, instill in me an unwavering belief as I come to You in prayer. May doubt be replaced with steadfast faith, making me firm and unshakable even in the face of challenges.

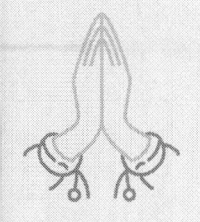

# Day 5: continuation

Scripture: Mark 9:24 (NIV) "Immediately the boy's father exclaimed, 'I do believe; help me overcome my unbelief!'"
Lord, like the desperate father in Mark 9:24, I declare my belief in You, yet acknowledge my human frailty. Extend Your divine help to overcome any lingering traces of unbelief within me.
Scripture: Ephesians 2:8-9 (NIV) "For it is by grace you have been saved, through faith—and this is not from yourselves, it is the gift of God—not by works, so that no one can boast."
Father, I understand that even faith is a gift from You. In humility, I receive this precious gift, recognizing that my salvation and the building of my faith are solely by Your grace.
Scripture: 1 Peter 1:7 (NIV) "These have come so that the proven genuineness of your faith—of greater worth than gold, which perishes even though refined by fire—may result in praise, glory and honor when Jesus Christ is revealed."
God, as my faith is tested and refined through the trials of life, let its genuineness shine forth. May the proven worth of my faith bring praise, glory, and honor to Your name.
Scripture: Romans 4:20-21 (NIV) "Yet he did not waver through unbelief regarding the promise of God, but was strengthened in his faith and gave glory to God, being fully persuaded that God had power to do what he had promised."
Lord, just as Abraham remained unwavering in faith, I seek the strength to fully trust in Your promises. May my faith be a source of glory and honor to You.
In the mighty name of Jesus, I pray.
                Amen.

SPACE FOR PERSONAL REFLECTIONS,
THOUGHTS, AND PRAYERS.

NOTES

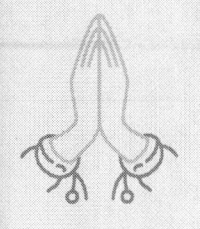

# Day 6 : Prayer for Personal Transformation

Adoration.
Start by praising God for who He is.
Songs: "Great Are You Lord" - All Sons & Daughters

Heavenly Father,
As I embark on this sacred journey of fasting and prayer, I surrender myself before Your throne, seeking a profound transformation within. Your promise in Romans 12:2 encourages me, "Do not conform to the pattern of this world, but be transformed by the renewing of your mind." Today, I purposefully choose to set aside the patterns of the world and invite Your transformative work in my life.

Scripture: Psalm 51:10 (NIV)"Create in me a pure heart, O God, and renew a steadfast spirit within me."
God, in the midst of fasting, I humbly ask for a profound inner transformation. Create within me a heart that reflects Your purity, and renew a steadfast spirit that remains committed to Your ways.

Scripture: 2 Corinthians 5:17 (NIV)"Therefore, if anyone is in Christ, the new creation has come: The old has gone, the new is here!"
Lord, I embrace the truth that, through Christ, I am a new creation. As I fast, let the old patterns and habits be replaced with the newness that comes from being in You.

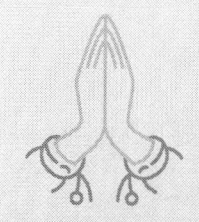

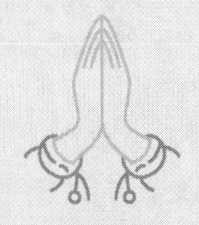

## Day 6: continuation

Scripture: Ephesians 4:22-24 (NIV)"You were taught, with regard to your former way of life, to put off your old self, which is being corrupted by its deceitful desires; to be made new in the attitude of your minds; and to put on the new self, created to be like God in true righteousness and holiness."
Father, during this time of fasting, I willingly lay aside my old self. Renew the attitude of my mind, and clothe me with the new self, reflecting Your righteousness and holiness.

Scripture: Colossians 3:10 (NIV)"and have put on the new self, which is being renewed in knowledge in the image of its Creator."
Lord, as I put on the new self, I pray for a continual renewal in knowledge. May I increasingly reflect the image of You, my Creator, in every aspect of my life.

Scripture: Philippians 1:6 (NIV)"being confident of this, that he who began a good work in you will carry it on to completion until the day of Christ Jesus."
God, I am confident that the good work You began in me will be carried to completion. In this time of fasting, continue Your transformative work until I fully reflect the likeness of Christ.
In the powerful name of Jesus, I pray.
Amen.

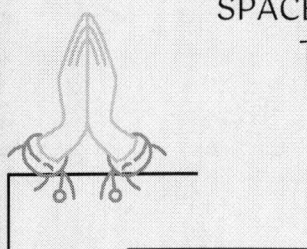

SPACE FOR PERSONAL REFLECTIONS,
THOUGHTS, AND PRAYERS.

NOTES

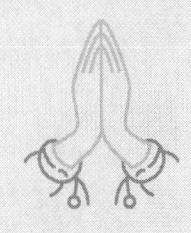

# Day 7 : Prayer for Wisdom and Guidance

Adoration.
Start by praising God for who He is.
Songs: "What a Beautiful Name" - Hillsong Worship

Heavenly Father,
As I embark on this season of fasting and prayer, I come before You with a heart seeking Your wisdom and guidance. Your Word in James 1:5 assures me, "If any of you lacks wisdom, you should ask God, who gives generously to all without finding fault, and it will be given to you." Lord, I acknowledge my need for Your divine wisdom and humbly seek Your guidance in every aspect of my life.

Scripture: Proverbs 3:5-6 (NIV)"Trust in the Lord with all your heart and lean not on your own understanding; in all your ways submit to him, and he will make your paths straight."
God, as I fast, I place my trust fully in You. I choose not to rely on my own understanding but to submit to Your guidance in all my ways. Straighten my paths, O Lord, according to Your perfect will.

Scripture: Psalm 32:8 (NIV)"I will instruct you and teach you in the way you should go; I will counsel you with my loving eye on you."
Father, during this fasting journey, I open my heart to Your instruction and teaching. Counsel me with Your loving eye upon me. May Your guidance be my constant companion.

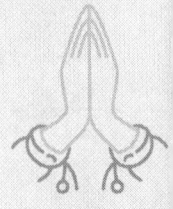

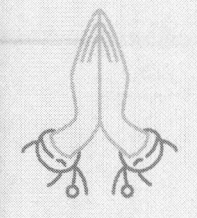

# Day 7: continuation

Scripture: Isaiah 30:21 (NIV)"Whether you turn to the right or to the left, your ears will hear a voice behind you, saying, 'This is the way; walk in it.'"
Lord, I long to hear Your guiding voice as I navigate through life. During this time of fasting, make Your direction clear to me. Whether I turn to the right or the left, may I discern Your voice saying, "This is the way; walk in it."

Scripture: Proverbs 16:3 (NIV)"Commit to the Lord whatever you do, and he will establish your plans."
God, as I commit my actions, plans, and decisions to You during this fast, I trust that You will establish them according to Your divine purpose. May my life align with Your will.

Scripture: Ephesians 1:17-18 (NIV)"I keep asking that the God of our Lord Jesus Christ, the glorious Father, may give you the Spirit of wisdom and revelation, so that you may know him better. I pray that the eyes of your heart may be enlightened in order that you may know the hope to which he has called you."
Father, I earnestly seek the Spirit of wisdom and revelation during this fasting season. Enlighten the eyes of my heart that I may know You better and understand the hope of Your calling.
Grant me discernment, O God, as I seek Your wisdom and guidance in this time of fasting. In the name of Jesus, who is the source of all wisdom, I pray.
Amen.

SPACE FOR PERSONAL REFLECTIONS,
THOUGHTS, AND PRAYERS.

NOTES

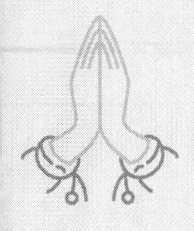

# Day 8 : Prayer for Health and Strength

Adoration.
Start by praising God for who He is.
Songs: "Amazing Grace (My Chains Are Gone)" - Chris Tomlin
Heavenly Father,

As I embark on this journey of fasting and prayer, I lift up my physical well-being to You. Your Word in 3 John 1:2 declares, "Beloved, I pray that all may go well with you and that you may be in good health, as it goes well with your soul." Lord, I seek Your divine touch on my health and strength during this time of fasting. Grant me the vitality needed to fulfill Your purposes.

Scripture: Psalm 41:3 (NIV)"The Lord sustains them on their sickbed and restores them from their bed of illness."
God, I trust in Your sustaining power. In moments of weakness, may Your divine touch bring restoration to my body. Uphold me on this fasting journey and strengthen me from any bed of illness.

Scripture: Isaiah 40:31 (NIV)"but those who hope in the Lord will renew their strength. They will soar on wings like eagles; they will run and not grow weary, they will walk and not be faint."
Father, as I put my hope in You, I ask for a renewal of strength. May I soar on wings like eagles, run without growing weary, and walk without fainting. Grant me endurance and resilience throughout this fasting period.

# Day 8: continuation

Scripture: 1 Corinthians 6:19-20 (NIV) "Do you not know that your bodies are temples of the Holy Spirit, who is in you, whom you have received from God? You are not your own; you were bought at a price. Therefore, honor God with your bodies."

Lord, I recognize that my body is Your temple. During this fast, I honor You with my body and seek Your divine intervention for health and strength. May my physical well-being glorify You.

Scripture: Psalm 73:26 (NIV) "My flesh and my heart may fail, but God is the strength of my heart and my portion forever."

God, I acknowledge my human limitations, but I rely on Your strength that transcends my own. Be the strength of my heart, and may You be my eternal portion. In moments of weakness, may I find strength in You.

Scripture: Exodus 15:26 (NIV) "He said, 'If you listen carefully to the Lord your God and do what is right in his eyes, if you pay attention to his commands and keep all his decrees, I will not bring on you any of the diseases I brought on the Egyptians, for I am the Lord, who heals you.'"

Lord, as I listen carefully to Your voice and align my life with Your commands during this fast, I trust in Your promise of healing. You are the Lord who heals, and I place my health in Your caring hands.

Grant me resilience, strength, and vibrant health as I undertake this period of fasting. May my physical well-being be a testament to Your goodness and sustaining power. In Jesus' name, I pray.     Amen.

SPACE FOR PERSONAL REFLECTIONS, THOUGHTS, AND PRAYERS.

NOTES

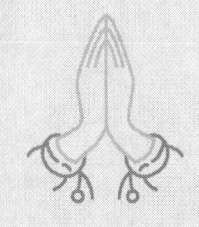

# Day 9 : Prayer for Family Unity

Adoration.
Start by praising God for who He is.
Songs: "Oceans (Where Feet May Fail)" - Hillsong UNITED
Heavenly Father,
As I enter into this time of fasting and prayer, I bring before You the bonds of my family. Your Word in Psalm 133:1 declares, "How good and pleasant it is when God's people live together in unity!" Lord, I lift up my family members to You, seeking Your divine intervention for unity, love, and understanding. Strengthen the ties that bind us and cultivate an atmosphere of harmony within our family.

Scripture: Colossians 3:13-14 (NIV)"Bear with each other and forgive one another if any of you has a grievance against someone. Forgive as the Lord forgave you. And over all these virtues put on love, which binds them all together in perfect unity."
God, grant us the grace to bear with one another and to forgive as You have forgiven us. Clothe us with the virtue of love, which binds all other virtues in perfect unity. May our home be a haven of forgiveness and love.

Scripture: Ephesians 4:2-3 (NIV)"Be completely humble and gentle; be patient, bearing with one another in love. Make every effort to keep the unity of the Spirit through the bond of peace."
Lord, instill in each family member humility, gentleness, and patience. Enable us to bear with one another in love, making every effort to maintain the unity of the Spirit through the bond of peace. May our home be a place of tranquility and understanding.

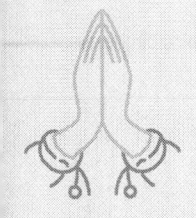

## Day 9: continuation

Scripture: Proverbs 17:17 (NIV)"A friend loves at all times, and a brother is born for a time of adversity."
Father, may our family be characterized by the love that endures all times. In moments of joy and challenges, let our bonds be unbreakable. Teach us to support and stand by each other, recognizing that we are born for times of adversity.

Scripture: Psalm 127:1 (NIV)"Unless the Lord builds the house, the builders labor in vain. Unless the Lord watches over the city, the guards stand watch in vain."
God, we acknowledge that true unity and strength come from You. As we fast and pray for our family, may our foundation be built by You. Watch over our home, and let Your presence be the cornerstone that holds us together.

Scripture: Romans 12:16 (NIV)"Live in harmony with one another. Do not be proud, but be willing to associate with people of low position. Do not be conceited."
Lord, guide our family to live in harmony. Remove pride and conceit from our midst, and instill in us a willingness to associate with humility and grace. May our interactions be filled with understanding and compassion.
May this time of fasting be a catalyst for unity within our family. Strengthen the ties that bind us, and let Your love be the foundation of our relationships. In Jesus' name, I pray.
Amen.

SPACE FOR PERSONAL REFLECTIONS, THOUGHTS, AND PRAYERS.

## NOTES

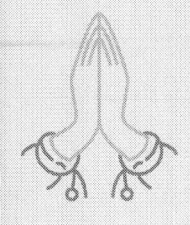

# Day 10 : Prayer for Financial Provision

Adoration.
Start by praising God for who He is.
Songs: "Goodness of God" - Bethel Music
Heavenly Father,
As I enter into this season of fasting and prayer, I bring before You the area of financial provision in my life. Your Word in Philippians 4:19 assures me, "And my God will meet all your needs according to the riches of his glory in Christ Jesus." Lord, I trust in Your promise to provide for my financial needs. Open doors of opportunity, bless the work of my hands, and grant me wisdom in stewarding the resources You provide.

Scripture: Malachi 3:10 (NIV)"Bring the whole tithe into the storehouse, that there may be food in my house. Test me in this,' says the Lord Almighty, 'and see if I will not throw open the floodgates of heaven and pour out so much blessing that there will not be room enough to store it.'"
God, as I honor You with my tithes and offerings during this fast, I trust Your promise to open the floodgates of heaven and pour out blessings beyond measure. May my financial obedience be met with Your abundant provision.

Scripture: Proverbs 3:9-10 (NIV)"Honor the Lord with your wealth, with the first fruits of all your crops; then your barns will be filled to overflowing, and your vats will brim over with new wine."
Lord, I choose to honor You with my wealth and the first fruits of my income. As I do so, I trust that my storehouses will be filled to overflowing, and Your abundance will flow into every aspect of my life.

# Day 10: continuation

Scripture: Matthew 6:33 (NIV) "But seek first his kingdom and his righteousness, and all these things will be given to you as well."
Father, as I fast and seek Your kingdom first, I believe that You will add all the necessary provisions to my life. Grant me the wisdom to prioritize Your kingdom, trusting that You will take care of my financial needs.

Scripture: 2 Corinthians 9:8 (NIV) "And God is able to bless you abundantly, so that in all things at all times, having all that you need, you will abound in every good work."
God, I declare Your ability to bless me abundantly. In every season and circumstance, provide for all my needs, enabling me to abound in every good work You've set before me.

Scripture: Deuteronomy 8:18 (NIV) "But remember the Lord your God, for it is he who gives you the ability to produce wealth."
Lord, I recognize that the ability to produce wealth comes from You. During this fast, guide me in using my talents, skills, and opportunities to generate income. May my financial endeavors be aligned with Your will.

Grant me financial provision, O Lord, as I surrender this area of my life to You in fasting and prayer. Open doors of opportunity and pour out Your abundance according to Your glorious riches in Christ Jesus. In His name, I pray. Amen.

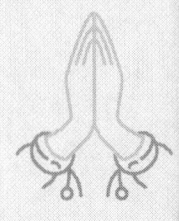

SPACE FOR PERSONAL REFLECTIONS,
THOUGHTS, AND PRAYERS.

NOTES

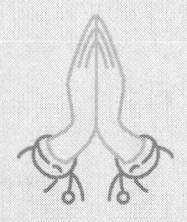

# Congratulations!!! On Completing 10 days!

During fasting, we're doing something special called "consecration." It's like setting aside a specific time just for connecting with God. This idea is similar to how priests, nuns, and monks in the Roman Catholic Church are set apart for serving God. Even church buildings are dedicated for spiritual purposes, like the special places in Jewish tradition. For the past seven days, lots of Christians worldwide have been dedicating this time for prayer and fasting. They're doing this to get closer to God and build a stronger relationship with Him. Another similar word is "sanctification," which means being set apart for holy purposes. When God led the Israelites out of Egypt, He told them, "I will take you as My people, and I will be your God." He wanted them to be different from others and focus on Him, promising good things if they followed His ways. As we continue fasting, it's a good idea to think about how God might be calling us, as individuals, to be different. We can ask the Holy Spirit to show us areas where we can align our lives with God's teachings.

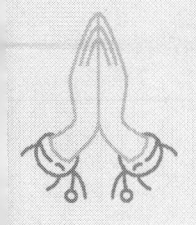

# You Are Almost there....!!!!

From the very first day of Daniel's fast, the Lord heard and responded to his prayer. However, a significant event occurred that holds valuable lessons for us. The prince of Persia hindered Daniel's blessings. Could a similar situation be hindering your blessings? As we began this fast, the Lord heard and answered, but it's essential to ensure that all blessings manifest here on earth in the name of Jesus. Nothing should be held up.

In Daniel's story, the angel explains his arrival and the opposition he faced from the Prince of the kingdom of Persia. This prince isn't a human but an evil angel, a demonic being. The New Testament recognizes organized demonic forces with a hierarchy, including principalities or "governments" associated with human governments. Jesus even referred to Satan as the prince of this world.

In prayer, Christians may face hindering factors unknown to them. It's crucial to persist in prayer, even when answers seem delayed. Jesus emphasized the significance of prayer and fasting in spiritual battles, teaching that men ought always to pray and not give up. As we continue this fast, let's persevere and overcome any hindrance, trusting in the power of prayer and fasting.

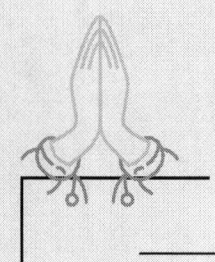

SPACE FOR PERSONAL REFLECTIONS, THOUGHTS, AND PRAYERS.

## NOTES

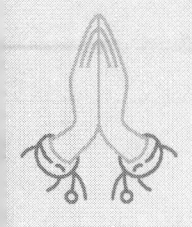

# Day 11 : Prayer for Joy Amid Challenges

Adoration.
Start by praising God for who He is.
Songs: "Build My Life" - Housefires

Heavenly Father,

As I enter into this season of fasting and prayer, I acknowledge that challenges may come, but Your Word assures me of the joy that surpasses circumstances. In James 1:2-3, it is written, "Consider it pure joy, my brothers and sisters, whenever you face trials of many kinds because you know that the testing of your faith produces perseverance." Lord, I seek the joy that can only be found in You, even in the midst of challenges. Grant me resilience, a steadfast spirit, and unwavering joy.

Scripture: Nehemiah 8:10b (NIV)"The joy of the Lord is your strength."
God, I recognize that true strength comes from the joy found in Your presence. As I fast and seek You, fill me with Your joy that empowers and sustains me in every circumstance.

Scripture: Psalm 30:5b (NIV)"Weeping may stay for the night, but rejoicing comes in the morning."
Lord, I understand that challenges may linger, but I hold onto the promise that joy will come. In the midst of weeping, I anticipate the morning of rejoicing. Your timing is perfect, and I trust in Your deliverance.

# Day 11: continuation

Scripture: Romans 15:13 (NIV)"May the God of hope fill you with all joy and peace as you trust in him, so that you may overflow with hope by the power of the Holy Spirit."
Father, as I trust in You during this fast, fill me with Your joy and peace. Let the hope that comes from Your Spirit overflow within me, even in the face of challenges. May my heart be anchored in Your unwavering joy.

Scripture: 2 Corinthians 4:16-18 (NIV)"Therefore we do not lose heart. Though outwardly we are wasting away, yet inwardly we are being renewed day by day. For our light and momentary troubles are achieving for us an eternal glory that far outweighs them all. So we fix our eyes not on what is seen, but on what is unseen, since what is seen is temporary, but what is unseen is eternal."
God, help me not to lose heart in the face of challenges. Let Your renewal happen within me day by day. May I fix my eyes on the eternal glory that far outweighs any temporary troubles, finding joy in Your eternal promises.

Scripture: Psalm 16:11 (NIV)"You make known to me the path of life; you will fill me with joy in your presence, with eternal pleasures at your right hand."
Lord, reveal to me the path of life and fill me with the joy that comes from being in Your presence. Let the assurance of eternal pleasures in Your right hand sustain me through every challenge I face during this fasting period.
Grant me a spirit of joy that remains unshaken by circumstances. In moments of difficulty, may the joy of the Lord be my strength and refuge. In Jesus' name, I pray.
Amen.

SPACE FOR PERSONAL REFLECTIONS,
THOUGHTS, AND PRAYERS.

## NOTES

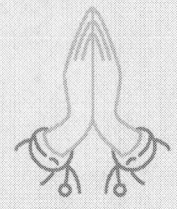

# Day 12 : Prayer for the Restoration of Dreams

Adoration.
Start by praising God for who He is.
Songs: "The Lion and the Lamb" - Leeland

Heavenly Father,
As I enter into this season of fasting and prayer, I bring before You the dreams and aspirations that may have been deferred or seem unreachable. Your Word in Joel 2:25 declares, "I will repay you for the years the locusts have eaten—the great locust and the young locust, the other locusts and the locust swarm—my great army that I sent among you." Lord, I trust in Your promise of restoration. I lay before You the dreams of my heart, seeking Your divine intervention and the fulfillment of Your purpose.

Scripture: Jeremiah 29:11 (NIV)"For I know the plans I have for you,' declares the Lord, 'plans to prosper you and not to harm you, plans to give you hope and a future."
God, I hold on to Your promise of plans for prosperity, hope, and a future. As I fast and seek Your face, align my dreams with Your divine purpose. May the desires of my heart be in harmony with Your perfect will.

Scripture: Psalm 37:4 (NIV)"Take delight in the Lord, and he will give you the desires of your heart."
Lord, I delight in You, and I trust that as I seek Your presence during this fasting period, You will grant the desires of my heart. Mold my desires to align with Your will, and let my dreams reflect Your glory.

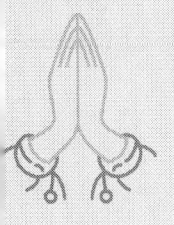

# Day 12: continuation

Scripture: Isaiah 43:19 (NIV)"See, I am doing a new thing! Now it springs up; do you not perceive it? I am making a way in the wilderness and streams in the wasteland."
Father, I look to You for a new thing. I believe that, even in seemingly barren places, You are making a way. Bring forth streams of opportunities and blessings in areas where my dreams may have faced obstacles.

Scripture: Psalm 20:4 (NIV)"May he give you the desire of your heart and make all your plans succeed."
God, I pray that You will give success to the plans and dreams of my heart. May Your favor rest upon the aspirations I hold dear. Let Your hand guide me towards the fulfillment of dreams aligned with Your purpose.

Scripture: Ephesians 3:20 (NIV)"Now to him who is able to do immeasurably more than all we ask or imagine, according to his power that is at work within us."
Lord, I trust in Your ability to do immeasurably more than I can ask or imagine. As I fast and seek Your face, let Your power work within me, bringing forth the restoration and fulfillment of dreams beyond my comprehension.
During this time of fasting, Lord, restore the dreams that may have been deferred or seemed out of reach. May my heart align with Your will, and may Your purpose be fulfilled in every dream and aspiration. In Jesus' name, I pray. Amen.

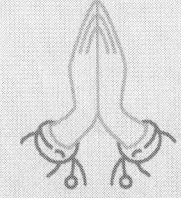

# SPACE FOR PERSONAL REFLECTIONS, THOUGHTS, AND PRAYERS.

# NOTES

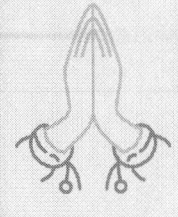

# Day 13 : Prayer for protecting your family

Adoration.
Start by praising God for who He is.
Songs: "Here I Am to Worship" - Tim Hughes
"Lord I Lift Your Name On High" - Hillsong

Heavenly Father,
I come before Your throne with a heart full of gratitude and a deep sense of responsibility for the protection of my family and loved ones. Your Word assures me of Your steadfast love and promises to shield those who trust in You.
Scripture: Psalm 91:11-12 (NIV) "For he will command his angels concerning you to guard you in all your ways; they will lift you up in their hands so that you will not strike your foot against a stone."
Lord, I claim the promises of Psalm 91 over my family. I trust that Your angels are dispatched to guard and protect them in every aspect of their lives.
Scripture: Proverbs 18:10 (NIV) "The name of the Lord is a fortified tower; the righteous run to it and are safe."
Father, I declare the name of the Lord as a fortified tower over my family. May they run to You and find safety in Your divine protection.
Scripture: Psalm 121:7-8 (NIV) "The Lord will keep you from all harm—he will watch over your life; the Lord will watch over your coming and going both now and forevermore."
God, I cling to the assurance that You keep my family from all harm. Watch over their lives, their daily activities, and their journeys, both now and forevermore.
Scripture: Isaiah 54:17 (NIV) "No weapon forged against you will prevail, and you will refute every tongue that accuses you.

# Day 13: continuation

This is the heritage of the servants of the Lord, and this is their vindication from me," declares the Lord."
Lord, I stand on the promise that no weapon formed against my family will prevail. Every accusation against them is refuted, for they are Your servants and bear Your vindication.
Scripture: Psalm 34:7 (NIV) "The angel of the Lord encamps around those who fear him, and he delivers them."
Father, I thank You for the angelic encampment around my family. Deliver them from all dangers, seen and unseen, as they fear and reverence You.
Scripture: Deuteronomy 31:6 (NIV) "Be strong and courageous. Do not be afraid or terrified because of them, for the Lord your God goes with you; he will never leave you nor forsake you."
God, instill strength and courage in my family. May the assurance of Your constant presence alleviate all fears, knowing that You will never leave nor forsake them.
Scripture: Psalm 46:1 (NIV) "God is our refuge and strength, an ever-present help in trouble."
Lord, be the refuge and strength of my family. As an ever-present help in trouble, may they find solace and safety in You.
Scripture: Ephesians 6:10-11 (NIV) "Finally, be strong in the Lord and in his mighty power. Put on the full armor of God, so that you can take your stand against the devil's schemes."
Father, I pray for each member of my family to be strong in You and to put on the full armor of God. Grant them discernment to stand against the schemes of the enemy.
In the powerful name of Jesus, I lift up this prayer for the protection of my family. Amen.

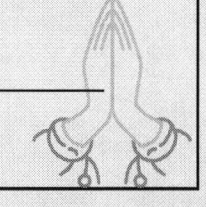

SPACE FOR PERSONAL REFLECTIONS, THOUGHTS, AND PRAYERS.

NOTES

# Day 14 : Prayer for Spiritual Discernment

Adoration.
Start by praising God for who He is.
Songs: "Holy Spirit" - Francesca Battistelli

Heavenly Father,
As I enter into this season of fasting and prayer, I recognize the importance of spiritual discernment. Your Word in Proverbs 3:5-6 encourages me to trust in You with all my heart and lean not on my own understanding, acknowledging You in all my ways for You to direct my paths. Lord, I seek Your wisdom and discernment during this time, that I may understand Your will and navigate the spiritual journey set before me.

Scripture: James 1:5 (NIV)"If any of you lacks wisdom, you should ask God, who gives generously to all without finding fault, and it will be given to you."
God, I come before You acknowledging my need for wisdom and discernment. I ask You, in faith, to generously grant me the discernment I seek. May Your wisdom guide my thoughts, decisions, and actions during this time of fasting.

Scripture: Hebrews 5:14 (NIV)"But solid food is for the mature, who by constant use have trained themselves to distinguish good from evil."
Lord, as I mature spiritually, help me to discern between good and evil. Through the constant practice of seeking Your Word and applying it, may my spiritual senses be finely tuned to distinguish what aligns with Your will.

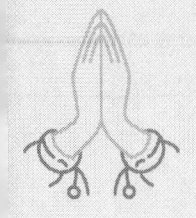

# Day 14: continuation

Scripture: 1 Corinthians 2:14 (NIV) "The person without the Spirit does not accept the things that come from the Spirit of God but considers them foolishness, and cannot understand them because they are discerned only through the Spirit."

Holy Spirit, open my spiritual eyes to discern the things that come from You. Guide me in understanding the deep truths of Your Word, for true discernment comes through Your revelation.

Scripture: Philippians 1:9-10 (NIV) "And this is my prayer: that your love may abound more and more in knowledge and depth of insight, so that you may be able to discern what is best and may be pure and blameless for the day of Christ."

Father, I pray for an abundance of love coupled with knowledge and insight. Grant me the ability to discern what is best, leading a life that is pure and blameless in Your sight.

Scripture: Colossians 1:9 (NIV) "For this reason, since the day we heard about you, we have not stopped praying for you. We continually ask God to fill you with the knowledge of his will through all the wisdom and understanding that the Spirit gives."

God, fill me with the knowledge of Your will. Grant me wisdom and understanding through the Holy Spirit, that I may discern the path You've set before me during this season of fasting.

May my spiritual discernment deepen as I seek Your face, and may I walk in alignment with Your perfect will. In Jesus' name, I pray.

Amen.

SPACE FOR PERSONAL REFLECTIONS,
THOUGHTS, AND PRAYERS.

## NOTES

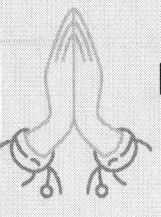

# Day 15 : Prayer for Protection from Evil

Adoration.
Start by praising God for who He is.
Songs: "No Longer Slaves" - Bethel Music
Heavenly Father,
As I embark on this season of fasting and prayer, I recognize the need for Your divine protection from the schemes of evil. Your Word in Psalm 91 assures me that those who dwell in the shelter of the Most High will rest in the shadow of the Almighty. Lord, I seek Your refuge and plead for Your protective covering during this time of fasting. Guard me against the assaults of the enemy and surround me with Your heavenly protection.

Scripture: Psalm 91:1-2 (NIV)"Whoever dwells in the shelter of the Most High will rest in the shadow of the Almighty. I will say of the Lord, 'He is my refuge and my fortress, my God, in whom I trust.'"
God, I choose to dwell in Your shelter and rest in Your shadow. You are my refuge and fortress, the One in whom I trust. I declare Your lordship over every aspect of my life during this season of fasting.

Scripture: Ephesians 6:12 (NIV)"For our struggle is not against flesh and blood, but against the rulers, against the authorities, against the powers of this dark world and against the spiritual forces of evil in the heavenly realms."
Lord, I acknowledge the spiritual battles that may arise during this time of fasting. Equip me with the full armor of God, that I may stand firm against the schemes of the enemy. Grant me discernment to recognize and resist the forces of darkness.

# Day 15: continuation

Scripture: James 4:7 (NIV)"Submit yourselves, then, to God. Resist the devil, and he will flee from you."
Father, I submit myself to You, recognizing Your authority. As I resist the devil, I trust that he will flee from me. Strengthen my resolve to stand firm against any evil influence that may try to hinder my spiritual journey.

Scripture: 2 Thessalonians 3:3 (NIV)"But the Lord is faithful, and he will strengthen you and protect you from the evil one."
God, Your faithfulness is my anchor. Strengthen me and protect me from the evil one. Let Your unwavering presence be a shield around me, preserving me from harm.

Scripture: Matthew 6:13 (NIV)"And lead us not into temptation, but deliver us from the evil one."
Lord, I pray the words Jesus taught us to pray. Lead me not into temptation but deliver me from the evil one. Preserve my heart and mind as I seek You during this time of fasting.
I trust in Your protective hand, O Lord, as I fast and seek Your face. Surround me with Your angels, and let Your light dispel every form of darkness. In the mighty name of Jesus, I pray.

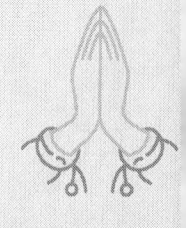

*Amen.*

## SPACE FOR PERSONAL REFLECTIONS, THOUGHTS, AND PRAYERS.

## NOTES

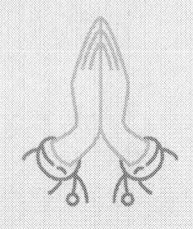

# Day 16 : Prayer for Release from Bondage

Adoration.
Start by praising God for who He is.
Songs: "Lord, I Need You" - Matt Maher

Heavenly Father,
As I enter into this season of fasting and prayer, I bring before You any areas of my life where I feel bound or entangled. Your Word declares in Isaiah 61:1 that You have sent Jesus to proclaim freedom for the captives and release from darkness for the prisoners. Lord, I seek Your divine intervention and liberation from any form of bondage that may hinder my spiritual journey. During this time of fasting, I ask for Your power to break every chain and set me free.

Scripture: Isaiah 61:1 (NIV)"The Spirit of the Sovereign Lord is on me, because the Lord has anointed me to proclaim good news to the poor. He has sent me to bind up the brokenhearted, to proclaim freedom for the captives and release from darkness for the prisoners."
God, I stand on the promise of Your Word that proclaims freedom for the captives. Let Your anointing break every chain that holds me captive. Release me from darkness and grant me the liberty that comes only through Christ.

Scripture: Galatians 5:1 (NIV)"It is for freedom that Christ has set us free. Stand firm, then, and do not let yourselves be burdened again by a yoke of slavery."
Lord, I declare that I am set free by the work of Christ on the cross. Help me stand firm in this freedom, resisting any attempts to be burdened again by the yoke of slavery. Grant me the strength to walk in the liberty You have provided.

# Day 16: continuation

Scripture: John 8:36 (NIV) "So if the Son sets you free, you will be free indeed."
Jesus, You are the Son who sets us free. I claim this promise, that in You, I am free indeed. Break the chains that bind me and lead me into the fullness of the freedom You offer.

Scripture: Romans 8:15 (NIV) "The Spirit you received does not make you slaves, so that you live in fear again; rather, the Spirit you received brought about your adoption to sonship. And by him, we cry, 'Abba, Father.'"
Holy Spirit, I embrace the adoption as Your child. Release me from any spirit of slavery and fear. Let the cry of my heart be, "Abba, Father," as I experience the freedom of being Your beloved.

Scripture: Psalm 146:7 (NIV) "He upholds the cause of the oppressed and gives food to the hungry. The Lord sets prisoners free."
Lord, uphold my cause as I seek release from any form of oppression. Like the prisoners You set free, let Your liberating power work in my life during this time of fasting.
Grant me the courage to let go of anything that hinders my freedom in You. May the chains be shattered, and may I walk in the glorious liberty that comes through the finished work of Christ. In His name, I pray.

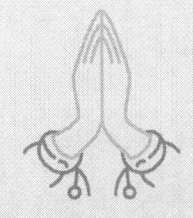

                     Amen.

SPACE FOR PERSONAL REFLECTIONS, THOUGHTS, AND PRAYERS.

NOTES

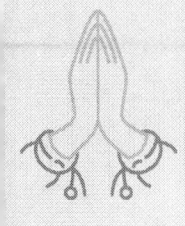

# Day 17 : Prayer for Making Healthy Relationship

Adoration.
Start by praising God for who He is.
Songs: "Tremble" - Mosaic MSC
"I Need You To Survive" - Hezekiah Walker

Heavenly Father,
As I embark on this sacred journey of fasting and prayer, I surrender myself before Your throne, seeking a profound transformation within. Your promise in Romans 12:2 encourages me, "Do not conform to the pattern of this world, but be transformed by the renewing of your mind." Today, I purposefully choose to set aside the patterns of the world and invite Your transformative work in my life.

Scripture: Psalm 51:10 (NIV) "Create in me a pure heart, O God, and renew a steadfast spirit within me."
God, in the midst of fasting, I humbly ask for a profound inner transformation. Create within me a heart that reflects Your purity, and renew a steadfast spirit that remains committed to Your ways.

Scripture: 2 Corinthians 5:17 (NIV) "Therefore, if anyone is in Christ, the new creation has come: The old has gone, the new is here!"
Lord, I embrace the truth that, through Christ, I am a new creation. As I fast, let the old patterns and habits be replaced with the newness that comes from being in You.

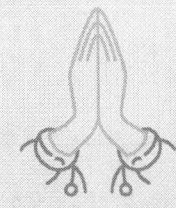

# Day 17: continuation

Scripture: Ephesians 4:22-24 (NIV) "You were taught, with regard to your former way of life, to put off your old self, which is being corrupted by its deceitful desires; to be made new in the attitude of your minds; and to put on the new self, created to be like God in true righteousness and holiness."
Father, during this time of fasting, I willingly lay aside my old self. Renew the attitude of my mind, and clothe me with the new self, reflecting Your righteousness and holiness.

Scripture: Colossians 3:10 (NIV) "and have put on the new self, which is being renewed in knowledge in the image of its Creator."
Lord, as I put on the new self, I pray for a continual renewal in knowledge. May I increasingly reflect the image of You, my Creator, in every aspect of my life.

Scripture: Philippians 1:6 (NIV) "being confident of this, that he who began a good work in you will carry it on to completion until the day of Christ Jesus."
God, I am confident that the good work You began in me will be carried to completion. In this time of fasting, continue Your transformative work until I fully reflect the likeness of Christ.
In the powerful name of Jesus, I pray for healthy relationships. May the purity of heart and the renewal of spirit manifest in my interactions with others.
Amen.

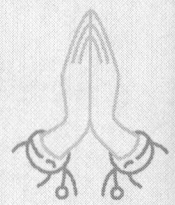

SPACE FOR PERSONAL REFLECTIONS,
THOUGHTS, AND PRAYERS.

NOTES

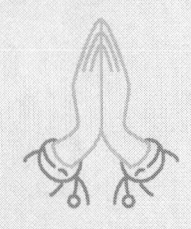

# Day 18 : Prayer for Fruitfulness in Ministry

Adoration.
Start by praising God for who He is.
Songs: "Living Hope" - Phil Wickham

Heavenly Father,
As I dedicate this season of fasting and prayer to You, I bring before You the ministry You have entrusted to me. Your Word in John 15:5 reminds me that apart from You, I can do nothing. Lord, I seek Your guidance, anointing, and divine favor upon this ministry. May it bear abundant fruit for Your glory. During this time of fasting, I surrender the ministry into Your hands, asking for Your transformative power.

Scripture: John 15:5 (NIV)"I am the vine; you are the branches. If you remain in me and I in you, you will bear much fruit; apart from me, you can do nothing."
God, I acknowledge my dependence on You. As the vine, I ask that You empower and guide every aspect of this ministry. Let it be a vessel that bears much fruit, bringing glory to Your name.

Scripture: Psalm 90:17 (NIV)"May the favor of the Lord our God rest on us; establish the work of our hands for us—yes, establish the work of our hands."
Lord, I seek Your favor to rest upon this ministry. Establish the work of our hands, that it may be aligned with Your will and purpose. Let Your divine favor open doors, draw hearts, and bring about impactful transformation.

# Day 18: continuation

Scripture: 1 Corinthians 15:58 (NIV)"Therefore, my dear brothers and sisters, stand firm. Let nothing move you. Always give yourselves fully to the work of the Lord, because you know that your labor in the Lord is not in vain."
Father, I stand firm in the commitment to this ministry. May our efforts be steadfast and unwavering. Assure us that our labor in the Lord is never in vain. May every seed sown result in a bountiful harvest.

Scripture: Isaiah 60:22 (NIV)"The least of you will become a thousand, the smallest a mighty nation. I am the Lord; in its time, I will do this swiftly."
Lord, fulfill Your promise in Isaiah 60:22 over this ministry. Let the impact multiply exponentially, from the least to a mighty nation. Swiftly bring about the growth and influence You desire for Your glory.

Scripture: Acts 1:8 (NIV)"But you will receive power when the Holy Spirit comes on you; and you will be my witnesses in Jerusalem, and in all Judea and Samaria, and to the ends of the earth."
Holy Spirit, I pray for an outpouring of Your power upon this ministry. Let it be a powerful witness, reaching not only locally but also to the ends of the earth. Equip us to be effective ambassadors for Christ.
May this time of fasting be a catalyst for spiritual growth, divine favor, and abundant fruitfulness in this ministry. I commit it into Your capable hands, trusting that You will bring about a harvest that glorifies Your name. In Jesus' name, I pray. Amen.

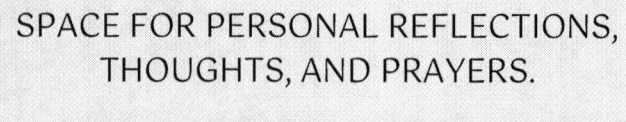

SPACE FOR PERSONAL REFLECTIONS, THOUGHTS, AND PRAYERS.

NOTES

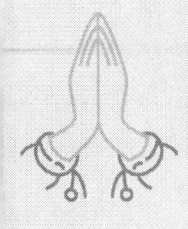

# Day 19 : Prayer for Provision and Miracles

Adoration.
Start by praising God for who He is.
Songs: "Raise a Hallelujah" - Bethel Music

Heavenly Father,
In this sacred time of fasting and prayer, I come before You with a heart full of gratitude for Your promise to provide for all our needs. Your Word in Philippians 4:19 assures us that You will meet all our needs according to the riches of Your glory in Christ Jesus. Lord, as I fast and seek Your face, I bring before You my needs, the needs of my loved ones, and those around me. I trust in Your abundant provision and anticipate the manifestation of miracles in our lives.

Scripture: Philippians 4:19 (NIV)"And my God will meet all your needs according to the riches of his glory in Christ Jesus."
Father, I claim the promise of Your provision. In this season of fasting, meet all our needs according to the vastness of Your glory in Christ Jesus. Be our Jehovah Jireh, our provider.

Scripture: Matthew 6:33 (NIV)"But seek first his kingdom and his righteousness, and all these things will be given to you as well."
Lord, as I seek Your kingdom first in this time of fasting, I trust that You will add all things unto us. Align our hearts with Your righteousness, and let provision flow in abundance.

# Day 19: continuation

Scripture: Luke 11:9-10 (NIV) "So I say to you: Ask and it will be given to you; seek and you will find; knock and the door will be opened to you. For everyone who asks receives; the one who seeks finds; and to the one who knocks, the door will be opened."
God, I come before You with my requests, seeking and knocking at the door of Your provision. I trust in Your willingness to give, and I anticipate the miraculous doors You will open during this time of fasting.

Scripture: 2 Corinthians 9:8 (NIV) "And God is able to bless you abundantly, so that in all things at all times, having all that you need, you will abound in every good work."
Lord, I believe in Your abundant blessings. Bless us in such a way that we have more than enough, enabling us to abound in every good work. Let our lives be a testimony to Your miraculous provision.

Scripture: James 1:17 (NIV) "Every good and perfect gift is from above, coming down from the Father of the heavenly lights, who does not change like shifting shadows."
Father, I acknowledge that every good and perfect gift comes from You. As I fast and pray, open the windows of heaven and pour out blessings and miracles that bring glory to Your unchanging nature.
During this season of fasting, let miracles unfold in unexpected ways. May Your provision be evident in every area of our lives, bringing joy and gratitude to our hearts. In the name of Jesus, I pray.
                    Amen.

SPACE FOR PERSONAL REFLECTIONS, THOUGHTS, AND PRAYERS.

NOTES

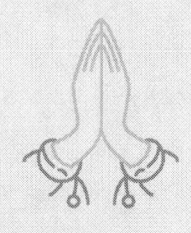

# Day 20 : Prayer for Gratitude and Contentment

Adoration.
Start by praising God for who He is.
Songs: "This is Amazing Grace" - Phil Wickham

Heavenly Father,
As I embark on this journey of fasting and prayer, I come before You with a heart filled with gratitude for Your unending goodness and faithfulness. Your Word in 1 Thessalonians 5:18 encourages us to give thanks in all circumstances. Lord, I choose to cultivate an attitude of gratitude and contentment during this time of fasting. Open my eyes to see the blessings around me and fill my heart with joy in Your presence.

Scripture: 1 Thessalonians 5:18 (NIV)"Give thanks in all circumstances; for this is God's will for you in Christ Jesus."
Father, I submit to Your will by giving thanks in all circumstances. During this period of fasting, help me recognize the countless blessings in my life, both big and small. Cultivate within me a heart that overflows with gratitude.
Scripture: Psalm 103:2-5 (NIV)"Praise the Lord, my soul, and forget not all his benefits— who forgives all your sins and heals all your diseases, who redeems your life from the pit and crowns you with love and compassion, who satisfies your desires with good things so that your youth is renewed like the eagle's."
Lord, I praise You and thank You for Your abundant benefits. During this fasting season, help me not to forget the forgiveness, healing, redemption, and satisfaction You provide. Crown me with Your love and compassion.

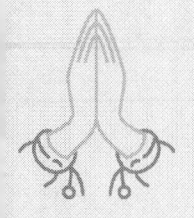

# Day 20: continuation

Scripture: Philippians 4:11-13 (NIV)"I am not saying this because I am in need, for I have learned to be content whatever the circumstances. I know what it is to be in need, and I know what it is to have plenty. I have learned the secret of being content in any and every situation, whether well fed or hungry, whether living in plenty or in want. I can do all this through him who gives me strength."

God, teach me the secret of contentment as the Apostle Paul learned. Regardless of my circumstances, whether well-fed or hungry, may I find strength in You and be content in the assurance of Your provision.

Scripture: Colossians 3:15 (NIV)"Let the peace of Christ rule in your hearts, since as members of one body you were called to peace. And be thankful."

Lord, may the peace of Christ rule in my heart during this fasting period. Instill within me a spirit of thankfulness, recognizing the unity and peace that come from being members of the body of Christ.

Scripture: Psalm 28:7 (NIV)"The Lord is my strength and my shield; my heart trusts in him, and he helps me. My heart leaps for joy, and with my song, I praise him."

Father, You are my strength and shield. As I trust in You during this fasting season, let my heart leap for joy, and may my song of praise be a melody of gratitude.

In the midst of fasting, let my heart overflow with gratitude and contentment. May this attitude of thanksgiving draw me closer to Your presence and deepen my appreciation for Your goodness. In Jesus' name, I pray.

Amen.

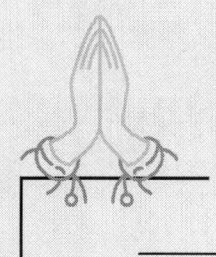

SPACE FOR PERSONAL REFLECTIONS,
THOUGHTS, AND PRAYERS.

NOTES

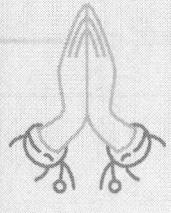

# Day 21 : Prayer of Thanksgiving for Answered Prayers

Adoration.
Start by praising God for who He is.
Songs: "Great Are You Lord" - All Sons & Daughters

Gracious Father,
I come before You with a heart overflowing with gratitude for the countless times You have answered my prayers. Your Word in Psalm 116:1-2 prompts me to declare, "I love the Lord, for he heard my voice; he heard my cry for mercy. Because he turned his ear to me, I will call on him as long as I live."

Verse: Psalm 116:1-2 (NIV) "I love the Lord, for he heard my voice; he heard my cry for mercy. Because he turned his ear to me, I will call on him as long as I live."
Lord, my heart rejoices in Your faithfulness. You have heard my cries, and Your mercy has been poured out upon me. I am eternally grateful for Your attentive ear and Your loving response to my prayers.

Verse: Philippians 4:6 (NIV) "Do not be anxious about anything, but in every situation, by prayer and petition, with thanksgiving, present your requests to God."
God, Your instruction in Philippians 4:6 has been my guide. I presented my requests to You with thanksgiving, and You, in Your boundless love, have graciously answered.
Verse: 1 Thessalonians 5:16-18 (NIV) "Rejoice always, pray continually, give thanks in all circumstances; for this is God's will for you in Christ Jesus."

## Day 21: continuation

Lord, I heed the call of 1 Thessalonians 5:16-18. In every circumstance, I choose to rejoice, pray continually, and give thanks for the answered prayers that manifest Your perfect will in my life.

Verse: Psalm 138:3 (NIV) "When I called, you answered me; you greatly emboldened me."
Father, as I reflect on the times I called upon Your name, I am filled with awe. You not only answered but also emboldened me with Your divine strength. I am thankful for the courage You have instilled in me through Your responses.

Verse: James 5:16 (NIV) "Therefore confess your sins to each other and pray for each other so that you may be healed. The prayer of a righteous person is powerful and effective."
God, I celebrate the powerful and effective nature of prayer, as described in James 5:16. Thank You for the healing, restoration, and breakthroughs that Your righteousness has ushered into my life.

Verse: Psalm 34:4 (NIV) "I sought the Lord, and he answered me; he delivered me from all my fears."
Lord, You are my deliverer. I sought You in moments of fear, and You answered, dispelling every fear that sought to paralyze me. I am thankful for Your constant presence.
May my heart forever echo with gratitude for the multitude of answered prayers. In Jesus' name, I offer this prayer of thanksgiving.

Amen.

SPACE FOR PERSONAL REFLECTIONS, THOUGHTS, AND PRAYERS.

NOTES

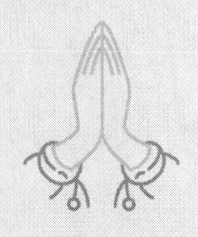

# Congratulations!!!
# You Completed 21 Days fasting & Prayers

Seek the Holy Spirit's intervention today, asking Him to uproot all vices within you and receive a new life from Almighty God. Command the devil and his cohorts to pack their luggage and vacate your home. Declare to the enemy that there is no room for him anymore; it's all filled up with the FRUITS of the Holy Spirit. Are you familiar with these FRUITS? They encompass LOVE, JOY, PEACE, PATIENCE, KINDNESS, GOODNESS, AND FAITHFULNESS. Let these virtues saturate your life, displacing any negative influence. With the Holy Spirit's power, make your family and affairs, including LESA, off-limits to the devil. Proclaim confidently that your space is reserved for the transformative presence of the Holy Spirit.

In Jesus fasting for 40 days and nights, we find profound inspiration. His journey through hunger, solitude, and temptation reveals the strength of the human spirit anchored in divine purpose. Amidst challenges, His unwavering commitment to God's will demonstrates resilience. As we face our own trials, remember His words: "Man shall not live by bread alone, but by every word that proceeds out of the mouth of God." Embrace the power of spiritual nourishment, finding sustenance in God's promises. Just as Jesus emerged victorious, let His fasting be a beacon, guiding us through life's wilderness toward triumph.

As you fast and pray, expect God's favor, guidance, and transformative power. The rewards may manifest differently for each, but the biblical narrative assures us of God's faithful response to earnest seeking.

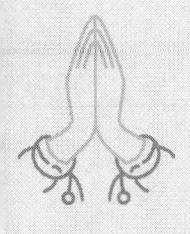

# Closing Prayer
# for 21 Days of Fasting and Prayer

Heavenly Father,
As we stand at the conclusion of these 21 days of fasting and prayer, our hearts overflow with gratitude for the journey we have undertaken in Your presence. Your Word reminds us in James 4:8, "Draw near to God, and he will draw near to you." Lord, we draw near to You with humble hearts, acknowledging that every step of this journey has been guided by Your loving hand.
Verse: James 4:8 (NIV) "Draw near to God, and he will draw near to you."
Thank You, Father, for the intimacy we have experienced with You during these 21 days. Your presence has been our constant companion, and we are grateful for the spiritual growth, breakthroughs, and revelations You have granted us.
As we conclude this sacred season, we reflect on the promises of Psalm 23:6, "Surely your goodness and love will follow me all the days of my life, and I will dwell in the house of the Lord forever." Lord, we carry the assurance that Your goodness and love will continue to accompany us on the journey ahead.
Verse: Psalm 23:6 (NIV) "Surely your goodness and love will follow me all the days of my life, and I will dwell in the house of the Lord forever."

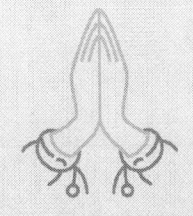

God, we offer our heartfelt thanks for answered prayers, for the times of testing that refined our faith, and for the moments of worship that brought us closer to Your heart. As we transition from this period of fasting, we commit ourselves to maintaining a posture of seeking You daily.

May the lessons learned, the spiritual disciplines cultivated, and the breakthroughs experienced during these 40 days bear lasting fruit in our lives. We pray for divine favor and direction for the days and months ahead.

Verse: Proverbs 3:5-6 (NIV) "Trust in the Lord with all your heart and lean not on your own understanding; in all your ways submit to him, and he will make your paths straight."

Lord, as we trust in You with all our hearts, we submit our plans, dreams, and aspirations to Your sovereign will. Make our paths straight, and guide us in the way of righteousness.

In closing, we express our deep gratitude for Your unwavering love, grace, and faithfulness. May Your peace, which surpasses all understanding, guard our hearts and minds in Christ Jesus.

Verse: Philippians 4:7 (NIV) "And the peace of God, which transcends all understanding, will guard your hearts and your minds in Christ Jesus."

Into Your hands, we commend the future, knowing that our times are in Your hands. In the precious name of Jesus, we offer this closing prayer.

Amen.

## REFLECT AND EVALUATE

## NOTES

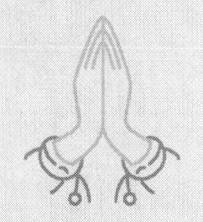

# Intellect Nourishment

We've been misled into thinking that prolonged prayer and fasting alone can make anything we desire materialize or vanish. But what about unresolved issues like unforgiveness, pride, envy, or, in essence, a life marred by sin? God is merciful, yet He is also a just God. The consequences of sin are severe, and adhering to God's commands brings blessings. To truly embrace the Kingdom lifestyle, we must grasp the operational principles of the Kingdom of God. Seeking the Kingdom and its righteousness doesn't mean neglecting other aspects of life. It signifies comprehending the Kingdom's principles for them to positively impact our lives. Without this understanding, merely reading the Word of God and acquiring knowledge won't bring about transformation or change.

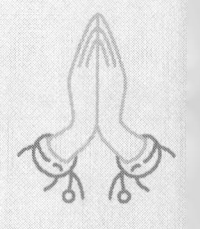

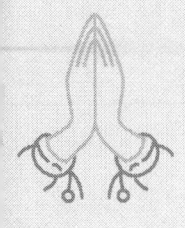

# Benefits of Prayer—No Matter the Outcome

In the Scriptures, Hannah fervently prayed for a child and was subsequently blessed with Samuel. Elijah prayed for rain, and rain was granted. Daniel sought divine insight to interpret dreams, and God responded positively.

Conversely, when Jesus prayed for relief from the impending torture and crucifixion, His request was not fulfilled. Paul prayed to be delivered from the "thorn" in his side but was granted the strength to endure it through divine grace.

Over the years, I've uttered numerous prayers. While some were fulfilled according to my desires, many remained unanswered. However, I've come to realize that irrespective of the response, there is still a gain. Interestingly, receiving the answer I anticipated is seldom the most significant outcome or the ultimate benefit of prayer. As I contemplate the moments and effort invested in prayer, I discern seven ways in which I've profited, irrespective of the end result:

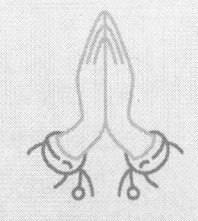

**Silence.** There are instances when it seems I'm enveloped, perhaps even bombarded, by incessant noise. Yet, through prayer, moments of stillness grace my life, becoming a source of solace for my soul. In prayer, I frequently find myself echoing the sentiment of being "calmed and quieted... like a weaned child with its mother" (Psalm 131:2 NIV).

**Tranquility.** Likewise, the moments I spend in prayer transform into a sanctuary amidst the perpetual hustle of my heart, mind, and body. While I may not precisely gauge the impact of prayer on averting or alleviating stress, anxiety, high blood pressure, and the like, I am assured that it has played a significant role. Philippians 4:6-7 (NIV).

**Connection.** There are those who journey through their entire existence without embracing (or recognizing) the presence of God. My life would lack richness if I neglected prayer and missed the profound joy of connecting with His presence (refer to Psalm 16:11).

**Shift in Focus.** While my prayers may not always yield the desired answers, they consistently provide a fresh perspective. Challenges appear less daunting, priorities become clearer, and the future seems more defined. In these moments, God's greatness becomes more apparent. Isaiah 40:31 (NIV).

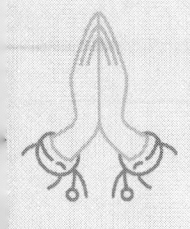

# Benefits of Prayer—No Matter the Outcome

**Equilibrium**. I resonate with the psalmist's words: "As for me, my feet had almost slipped; I had nearly lost my foothold" (Psalm 73:2 NIV). Striking a balance in life is challenging, and it's easy to veer off course, reacting to external pressures and teetering on the emotional edge. Yet, through prayer, I find reorientation—a realignment. Holding onto God's hand, I regain my balance, echoing the psalmist's sentiment: "But as for me, it is good to be near God" (Psalm 73:28 NIV).

**Peace.** The combined impact of silence, stillness, the presence of God, a renewed perspective, and restored balance through prayer is challenging to articulate or measure. However, I can affirm that with increased prayer, I encounter the fulfillment of Isaiah 26:3: "You will keep in perfect peace all who trust in you, all whose thoughts are fixed on you!" (NLT).

**Hope.** The consistency of my prayers ensures an enduring sense of hope. The anticipation of healing, deliverance, blessings, and goodness takes residence in my soul, steadfast through every storm. Even in instances where the anticipated outcome may not materialize, the realization that my benevolent God is perpetually at work, orchestrating something even more magnificent, uplifts my heart and soul. Romans 15:13 (NIV).

## REFLECT AND EVALUATE

## NOTES

## REFLECT AND EVALUATE

## NOTES

Made in the USA
Columbia, SC
27 June 2024